Flying to the Stars

Ronald Hyatt

SOPHOS BOOKS

Flying to the Stars

Published by
Sophos Books
Croydon
sophosbooks.com

ISBN 978-1-917960-25-0

Cover design by Tope Enoch
Printed in the United Kingdom

Contents

To my children,
their children, and their children's children.
May I see you all in glory land.

Acknowledgements

First, I want to give God praise for allowing me to write this book. Without Him, we cannot do anything. As I have stated many times before, I am glad when I answered the call to surrender my life to God, and I am encouraging all who read this book to give their lives to Him. You will rejoice and be glad you did so.

I want to thank my wife who has given over sixty years of her life to take care of me.

Although my parents are deceased, I thank God for them teaching me to know that there is a God, and we should honour Him all the days that we are alive.

To all my children: I want you to know that I love you all and I am praying for you, your children, and your children's children. Just as you have one father, so does God have one heavenly Son. As you loved your parents, do so more to God. I love you all, but God loves you more than I do.

I want to thank all who have shown me kindness all the days of my life. All you did for me was done also for God. His love far outweighs that of anyone else.

I want to thank Dr Sharon McLean, who helped me to proofread this book and my other books.

It gives me the honour to thank the publisher who has agreed to publish this book and others that I may write. May the business be blessed abundantly, now and in the future.

God bless you all in this world and the one to come.

CHAPTER 1

Flying to the Stars

When we look into the skies, we see countless stars. We are told there could be millions of them. Yes, they are up there, but how did they get there, and how can we reach them?

There are those who believe that every man and woman is born under a star sign. But who put the stars in the sky, and what is their purpose?

In the Holy Bible, we are told that God has numbered every star, and He knows their purpose. What would have happened if these stars were not in position? Our Heavenly Father knows the reason why He placed them in the heavens.

During my childhood days, when you looked up in the sky and saw these bright stars, they were so beautiful and elegant. To reach these stars or get a closer look, it felt as though you would need wings to fly up to the heavens.

I remember a song that went like this: *"If I had wings like a dove, I would fly away, fly away..."*

There must be a reason why one would wish to fly away, and perhaps only the individual knows the reason.

In the days of slavery, I heard that the slaves who refused to work would be taken away by night to be killed. When, on the following day, the other slaves inquired about their whereabouts, they were told that those slaves had flown away to Africa because they did not like it in Jamaica.

This was a lie, and it was wicked for anyone to treat others like that. We will each have to give an account of our deeds in this life.

I believe God impressed it upon my heart to write *Flying to the Stars*. I pray it helps you, dear reader, to take another look at yourself and make changes where necessary in your lifestyle, because He who created us did so for a good reason. I also pray that you will be blessed.

CHAPTER 2

Live by Faith

Faith is the evidence of things not yet seen, and hope for things yet to come (Hebrews 11:1). You cannot live in this world without having faith.

When I was young, our district in Jamaica was in a valley, with a hill on the southern side. When you climbed this hill, you would find level ground, fit for a football pitch. I climbed this hill many times. I had to climb it to milk a cow and take it to where the milk truck would collect it at 6am in the morning.

There were times when I wish I could pray and have faith that this hill would move and become level, of course this was when I was a child.

In the old days, it would have been very difficult for our forefathers to travel abroad. There were no planes, so it would have to be by ship or boat and would take quite a while to reach one's destination.

When the two brothers with the surname Wright first invented an airplane, everyone laughed at them. Today, however, we can travel to any part of the world.

My mother told me that when I was a child, I was terrified by the sound of a plane and would run to hide under the bed. In those days, the base of the bed was high enough for you to go under it. I remembered the last time I did that. I was about four years old.

In my younger days, I could only hope that one day I would be able to travel on a airplane. I was poor, with no income to support myself.

Between 1954 and 1955, I had a vision that I was travelling on a ship. On another time, I dreamed I was travelling on a plane. In 1956, I boarded a plane to America. Not long after, I took a flight to the United Kingdom. I have since travelled by airplane to many countries, including the Holy Land, Israel.

By faith, you can do anything. You can move mountains. Nothing is too small or too large. You can achieve your goals. As long as you have faith, it shall be done.

In the Bible we read that Peter told the crippled man: *"Silver and gold we have none, but in the name of Jesus Christ get up, take up your bed and walk"* (Acts 3:6).

To do such a miracle, you need to have a close relationship with God the Father and His Son, Jesus Christ. You can reach the greatest heights, and even take your flight to any country you desire.

We were all put here on this planet to multiply. This does not only mean having children. In this world, you need houses to live in, transportation to take you to and from places. You will need to have a reasonable income - unless you inherited a lump sum of cash or investments.

It is not a sin to have wealth, but it is a sin if you make it your god. We are told we should have no other God than the Heavenly Father, the God who created us.

Birds have two wings. How good it would be if we had wings to travel with! You never know – maybe one day, someone may invent wings we could use, just as you use a car!

CHAPTER 3

Prepare and Plan Well

A plane needs a pilot to navigate its course in the sky. It may be possible in the future to have planes flying without a pilot, but for now this is not the case.

Before you can travel on a plane, you need your travel documents, including your passport and boarding pass. In some countries, you will also need a visa. Your luggage must also be within the correct weight before you will be allowed to travel.

My advice to the younger generation is this: *Seek to reach new heights by being honest with yourself and others.*

When my children were growing up, they would come home asking why they could not have free school dinners like the other children whose parents were both working. I told them, *"Do not look at what other people have, because you do not know how they obtained it."*

As a child, I knew of a man who came to our district. Although he was from a very poor background, he worked hard and was able to build a large home there.

"How did he manage to do that?" you may ask.

He got the chance to travel to America, and he saved his income. That was how he became successful. Not long after, he bought a new motor truck.

To be able to fly to new heights, set your goals at a reasonable level. Be positive, and be honest. In one of my previous books (if you are able to get a copy), you will read how i described an experience I had because of my honesty.

We are in this world to do good to one another. King Solomon asked God for wisdom and understanding. Because of that request, riches were also added to him. *"Be wise as a serpent, but harmless as doves"* (Matthew 10:16).

"Study to show yourself approved, a workman worthy of the call, which is your reasonable service to God and man."

(2 Timothy 2:15)

Don't just sit back expecting things to fall into your lap. Things may not happen overnight, but rest assured, things will work out good for you if you try.

When I was a child, I heard a man say he was walking by the riverside when he heard some children singing, *"The Lord will provide..."*

This is very true. He will provide. Do not give up, and do not hide your talent.

CHAPTER 4

God is For You

A plane flying without passengers is a waste of energy and time, unless it was specifically intended to do so.

Once a plane takes off, you are suspended between life and death, with no assurance that you will land safely. We can only hope so. Once, I was travelling to Jamaica with my wife and there was a turbulent storm. A lady was sitting beside us, and all three of us began praying for safe landing. It was a deeply uncomfortable journey.

The first time I boarded a plane was in June 1956, when I took a flight to America. It was so exciting to travel over the Caribbean Sea! On our return to Jamaica the following year, as we flew back over the sea, we began singing, *"Home once more... the prodigal son returned to his home once more."* Over the loudspeaker, the pilot joined in.

Even if you are born into wealthy a family, make plans for yourself like your parents may have done. Blessed is the child who can stand on their own!

Your mother and father owe you nothing beyond caring for you until you are old enough to care for yourself. What they possess is theirs, and it is up to them to decide what is to be done with their legacy.

If they do wish to leave you an inheritance, make good use of it, and remember to share with relatives and to a charity.

Flying to the stars requires good planning. It is also important to have someone who can help guide you along the way. There are people who will go out of their way to hinder your success in life.

I was given the chance to learn engineering at a factory in Jamaica at eighteen, nearing nineteen years old. A young man went to the supervisor and reported that I was over eighteen years old. I was not yet nineteen, but out of spite, he did that and I lost the chance to do my apprenticeship.

We read in the Holy Book how Joseph's brothers sold him into slavery out of jealousy. Yet in God's timing, that very position enables him to save them from famine. Joseph had dreamed that his brothers would one day bow before him, and because of that dream, they hated him.

These things are still happening, but if God is for you, no weapon from hell can stop you from flying high. Just keep trusting God and He will make a way for you. Your enemies will be amazed at how you are getting through.

The heart of man is desperately wicked, but with God by your side, you will move mountains. Keep your eyes on the One who made heaven and earth. Your enemies will become your friends as the years go by, so never give up!

We are all here on this planet earth for a purpose. The person who is against you today is the one who you may have to rescue tomorrow. Throughout my time on this earth, I have seen the many ways people are treated, but God sees us and He will reward all those who have done good or bad to others.

Therefore, seek to do good to others, and strive to achieve new heights each day. If one door closes, another will surely open.

CHAPTER 5

The Great Pilot

I am waiting to board that heavenly plane, whose Captain and Pilot will be Jesus Christ, the Son of God. You are invited to get on board. All you need is to be washed in the blood of the Lamb, Jesus Christ, and to be found living a good Christian lifestyle.

You cannot make it on your own without God. It is simply not possible. It is only possible when you give your life to Him. There won't be any need for seat belts on this journey, for you will be in good hands while you are travelling to your destination, which is heaven. On arrival, after being welcomed by the angels, you will be taken to the mansion that Jesus had prepared for you.

You will not be disturbed by fellow passengers, for all are washed by the blood of Jesus Christ. I recall once travelling from Jamaica, after visiting my family and friends. On that flight, I was so disturbed by a passenger that a stewardess had to move me to another seat. This was the plan of Satan (you may read my book, *The Life of R.L. Hyatt,* where I narrate this story in full).

On this heavenly plane, the devil won't be allowed to do you any harm. The angels will be there to protect you from all evil.

Jesus Christ walks with me and talks to me. He tells me I am His own, What an assurance – to know that you are protected by God and his Son, Jesus Christ.

What a friend! What a precious friend! He walks with me, He talks with me, and He tells me I am His own. To have such a friend is true comfort.

When planning to travel on a plane, you need to know that the owner is well reputable, and their records are of a good standing. You do not want to be stranded in a foreign land without a way home. But the flight you are taking with Jesus Christ, the Son of God, as the pilot is a one-way ticket. You won't return to where you once belong.

In this life, there are many ups and downs, but with God by your side, you will surely make it. Stay strong, and put your trust in the true and living God who has never lost a battle.

There is no God like my God. His way is the only way. Generations of old placed their trust in him, and He never failed them. Stay close to him and surely, He will make away for you.

On the heavenly plane, you are not allowed to carry excess weight. You must lay aside every weight that will cause you to fall. Anger, malice and hatred will prevent you from boarding that heavenly plane.

CHAPTER 6

Don't Miss Your Flight

Missing your flight on this heavenly plane something you will live to regret, because you will miss the everlasting life promised by God.

"God, please give me wings so that I will fly away and be at home with friends who are waiting for me."

The angels are waiting to show us the mansions that have been prepared for us. They will fold their wings when they hear us singing, *"Hallelujah! Glory to God!"* Oh, what joy that will be!

The devil is a liar and a thief. He is after your soul. Do not allow him to take it away from you. You too can enjoy all the good things awaiting those who surrender their lives to God, the Father of us all. His son will be coming back, so be ready to meet Him.

What will your answer be if you miss this heavenly flight? You, and you alone, are responsible for every deed done on this side of life. You only have one chance, so, take good action now while it is day. Be wise. Choose wisely while there is time!

In my youth in Jamaica, we often sang, *"If I have wings like a dove, I would fly away from my troubles and be at home at last."*

We were living in the western part of the Island and when winter approached, a certain species of birds would fly somewhere to escape the winter months. Some people believed they were on their way to Africa. Who knows? This could well be the case.

If it were possible for humans to have wings to fly, would there be a tax to pay or some other levy imposed? The jury is still out on this one, and we can only wait for future inventions! However, what we do know is that there won't be any landing tax on the heavenly flight. All taxes have already been paid by the blood of Jesus Christ. He paid it all on the day He was crucified.

Having wings to fly would have been an advantage: we would go to places easily. Nevertheless, the Heavenly Father knows why He did not give humans wings.

Planning an earthly flight is not always easy. Someone could be trying to get rich from your intended travel.

We are capable of almost anything. It was very disappointing when man failed God. If only Adam had obeyed God's command not to eat the forbidden fruit! Yet, He loves us with an everlasting love. It was because this love that He sent His Son to die for our sins. He has provided a way of escape from sin by the shedding of His Son's blood on the cross.

CHAPTER 7

What Do You Live For?

When God made man, He was very pleased. We are told in the Holy Book that He would come down in the cool of the day to have a chat with Adam. But one day, God came, and Adam was not in his usual place. He was hiding from God. Imagine hiding from the One who created you! You cannot hide from God; He knows every step you take.

Come let us reason together. If heaven is real, why do you want to stay in this world? In this life – and you only have one – you may live as I have: over 90 years and still going on, or you may not be blessed as I am. King David said in Psalms 91:16, *"With long life I shall satisfy him and show him my salvation."* Here we are. I am a living proof of God's salvation.

Yes, I have lived to see ninety years and beyond, and I give God thanks for granting me such a long life. None of my grandparents were able to live so long. Still, if our only hope was in this life, how miserable that would be.

You were born into a good family, got a good education, got a good job and got married. You get to buy a lovely house, build up a large investment, then retire with the hope of living happy for a few years. Then suddenly, news reaches your family that you've had an accident and died.

Here we are. You have worked all these years, but you have not lived to enjoy your retirement years. This is the reality: you have no control over how long you live.

In this life, there is no hope of future events. You came with nothing, and you will leave with nothing.

Your only true hope is to surrender your life to God, to serve Him with all your heart. Then, when you die, you will have a certainty that you will be on that heavenly flight to eternal life, and you are guaranteed of having a better life after death. If it were not so, Jesus would have told us.

"Do not let your heart be troubled, I have gone to prepare a mansion for you and will come again to receive you unto myself."

(John 14:1-3)

Life is too short to worry about what you should eat and drink. I once heard of a woman who built an eighteen-room home with eighteen bathrooms for herself and her husband. The husband died and she got married to another man who was also rich, but he too died. This woman decided she did not want to live in the house anymore and sold it, moving into a one-bedroom apartment.

What am I living for, if it is not for God? Why would you have a large house, have millions of pounds or dollars in your bank account, yet you may not live to enjoy it?

Your soul is too precious to not take steps to ensure that when you depart this life, you will not find yourself in hell.

Be wise! It will be of no use, at the end of your life, to find yourself condemned with the devil and his angels. A better way has been made for you and I.

Mankind does not have any right to live, because we have rebelled against Him and have not turned our lives over to him. As from my young age, I heard it said that God never make mistakes, but He said in the bible, "I regret making man." We are the only living things that do not please God.

The whole duty of man is to serve God and keep His commandments, but we are rebellious, seeking to do whatever pleases us. Some of us take no responsibility for our actions. A day is coming, however, when we will have to give an account of all that we have done, whether good or evil.

When I came to the United Kingdom, I once sat on a bus speaking with a white man. In our discussion, I mentioned that anyone who fails to serve God will be going to hell, even our Queen at the time.

He asked me, *"You mean our Queen who is head of the Church of England, will be going to hell?"*

I replied in the affirmative. It does not matter who you are; you must be born again to enter the Kingdom of God. There are no exceptions!

Our last Queen was such a wonderful lady (God bless her!), and she did have Christian beliefs. We were even honoured to receive a signed certificate from her shortly before she died, congratulating us on sixty years of marriage. It is surely hoped she made it into heaven where we shall meet her again. Such a blessed woman!

Surely, you too will be glad to meet her again when we take our flight and enter eternal rest with God. Heaven is not only for the rich or poor, it is for *whosoever calls upon the Lord*.

There is hope for everyone, rich or poor. A song we usually sing says, *"You can have the whole world, but give me Jesus"*. It is of no use to have millions of pounds in the bank and lose your soul. We get caught up with the things of this world, craving for all the pleasures in the world. Some will even kill others to get what they want, forgetting that all this world's prosperity is only for a while.

Heaven is real. So is hell.

CHAPTER 8

His Time, Not Ours

Look at the world we are living in today. Is it worth it to desire only life on this earth?

There is a saying: *"The world is going too fast. I want to get off..."* Each day seems to be speeding by so quickly! When I was a child, it felt the opposite – the days seemed never-ending!

We are told in the Holy book, *"For the elect's sake, I will shorten the days..."* We should look up because our redemption draws near. It gives me great joy to invite all who are reading this book to consider starting a good relationship with God and His Son, Jesus Christ.

You have nothing to lose and everything to gain. Over the past six years, my health has been very poor. Prayers have been offered for my healing - to no avail. At times, it seems

God is far away. Nevertheless, Job said, *"Though he slays me, I will yet trust him."* My illness, I believe, serves a purpose.

If I had not been unwell, perhaps I would not have been able to write this book. This is my third book. I endeavour to share my life's story with all who will read this book and the other books I have written.

I want to encourage everyone: take courage, and be faithful to both God and man.

When I began serving God at an early age, I had very little. I was poor and had no income coming in. I owned only one good shirt, one good pair of trousers, and one good jacket. Nevertheless, I wore those garments to church without fail, sometimes barefoot.

Some years ago, I reflected on those days and a voice said to me, *"Because you were faithful to God, going to church, even going barefoot with only one shirt, I am now blessing you."* God will take care of all those who faithfully serve him.

In my local church in Jamaica, there seemed to be no blessing among the members. Many of us young people did not have jobs that allowed us to earn a living, and none of us could get married. Worse still, the young women were hesitant to marry young men who did not have a decent income to support both their wives and future families once they had children.

Then our local pastor at the time called a thirty-day fast, and not only did all the young people get married, we also built a brand-new church.

Yes, God does answer prayers – but always in His time, not ours. The Israelites had to wait four hundred years, but in the end, God said to Moses, *"Go and tell my people, I have heard their cry, and I have come down to deliver them."*

CHAPTER 9

Put Your Trust in God

After we leave our mother's womb, everything is against us. Our parents have a duty to care for us up to a certain age, yet some even refuse to take care of their children and put them up for adoption.

There are fathers who refuse to support the mothers of their children and expect those same children to care for them in old age – when their lives could be in danger and there is little they can do to help themselves.

Man is like a flower: today he is bright and beautiful, tomorrow, he fades away.

The best thing you can do is to put your life in the hands of the One who made you. He never fails, and His love for you is everlasting. *"Come unto me all who labour, and I will give you rest"* (Matthew 11:28).

When I was growing up, I did not know how my future would turn out. My father told me he was sorry he had not done his best to help. Yet, by the grace of God, I have done my best to make the most of my life. I was fortunate to find a good wife and to own three homes in the United Kingdom, albeit on mortgage. I am blessed with six children, eight grandchildren and three great- grandchildren.

However, I have done it only by the grace of God! He is truly the best companion you could have in this life.

I had a grand-aunt, a lovely woman who would always say to me, *"Put your trust in God"*. She was right. Bless her soul. My father did not give me much support, but I love him dearly and would love to hear him pray again with that lovely voice once again. I hope to meet him when this life is over and I take my flight to our heavenly home.

About eighteen of us were born in the same year as I was, and to the best of my knowledge, I am the only one still alive. My father had about ten children, and I am the only one alive. Perhaps God has spared me so that I might write this book to invite you to give your life to Him.

Come and join me in journeying to a place where we will never die and there will be no debt to pay. All has been paid by the blood of Jesus Christ when he hung on the cross to set us free.

Someday, I shall say goodbye to the world. I can't stay here much longer. I am going home to be with my Lord and saviour who gave His life for all men. He came to earth to die for me. What could be better than accepting Him and serving Him?

CHAPTER 10

Time is Running Out

I am a ready writer, eager to encourage all to give their lives to the one who died for them. Make no mistake: Jesus is the only one who can set you free from sin. He died to give us life, and without Him you will be lost in hellfire.

Hell was never meant for you. It was prepared for the devil and his angels. Why serve someone who cannot save himself? Jesus has loved you with an everlasting love – so much that He went on that cruel cross and shed His blood for you.

If it was possible for Him, maybe He would not have died on that cross. He said, *"Not my will"*, because it was the will of His Father. I have been to the Holy Land and seen the very sites where our Saviour was tried and convicted.

God so loved the world that He sent His only son to die on that cross so that we may live. He has promised to return one day, but are you prepared to meet him? Take courage, and join the millions who have already accepted Him as Lord and Saviour.

God is mighty to save. He loves us beyond measure, and what He has promised, He will surely do. You can take Him at His word. He is not like men, who would make you a promise but fail to honour their word.

When Jesus was born, Herod told the wise men, *"Go and search for him and when you have found him, come and tell me that I may also go and worship him"*. But he was not telling the truth. He had no desire to worship Jesus. He wanted to kill Him.

This is a very wicked world, and you may not know all those who secretly plan to harm you. I once heard of a woman who had worked abroad and sent money to her son to build a house. She decided to travel to see it. At the airport, she was met by a man with a gun. He asked her name to confirm her identity. When she did, he showed her the gun and the money he had been paid. He told her to take the next flight home, because her own son had hired him to kill her.

If a son can behave like that, who can you trust? Truly, as the saying goes, you dare not trust your own.

Over the years, I have spoken to many young women. They would say to me, *"You are a man. How come you are talking as you do?"* I could discern that they would be willing to have an affair with me, but I always made it clear that I am a Christian.

Some men tell women that they are not married so they can lure them into relationships. Likewise, there are women who are glad to hear a man tell them they are no more in love with their wives or girlfriends.

A woman once told me that she was in a relationship with a man who had told her he did not have any children. She later found out he was telling lies. He had children both in this country and abroad. God hates lies, and He will judge liars.

This world is full of deception and disappointment. You can have a solid plan, but then something unexpected happens, and your plans go out the window! I remember setting up a good investment plan to help with my retirement. Suddenly, I fell ill and was unable to work for about twelve months. I also had a cousin who always believed in having a secure future. He built a lovely home with hopes of retiring comfortably, returning to his homeland, and enjoying his life. Tragically, death took him away before he could realise those dreams. It's very sad!

CHAPTER 11

God Will Provide

I worked at a job for twenty-eight years. At the end of each year, I would look at my pension statements and feel reassured that, when I retired, I would have an income in addition to my state pension. Then, suddenly, news came that we were to be made redundant - and I still had a good number of years before retirement. I also had a mortgage to pay.

How was I going to manage? What was life going to be like? I had no answers, but God knew the future. Two little children were once walking down by the river side, praising God and singing, *"The Lord will provide..."* That is the answer to our fears.

Don't let this world and its problems get you down.

I heard of a woman who had no food to cook for her family, but went into her kitchen, put a cooking pot full of water on the stove and waited, hoping someone would come and provide food for her and her children.

I can confirm that God does provide. I mentioned earlier how I fell ill and was off work. In those days, I did not get paid while on sick leave. A sister from church phoned to find out how we were, and my wife told her I was off work because I was ill. This sister became concerned and asked my wife to tell me to come to her house. When I arrived, she had gathered many groceries worth over £40 (this was over forty years ago). After I got home, she called again to say she also had a large portion of beef, and I should come for it.

Our fore-parents went through a lot to make this world a better place to live. Some of the things that they put up with would shock us today, because we would never tolerate such hardship.

Still, there are more rivers to cross. Just tarry a little longer. Better days are coming, so let's keep our faith in God.

The Israelites waited four hundred years for God to deliver them. We have now waited more than two thousand years for Jesus to return, but He will be coming back to take us on that flight, and we will be singing, *"Home at last, Home at last"!* Be courageous.

Pause from reading this book for five minutes. Shut your eyes and think about the life you are living now. Ask yourself, *"What am I living for? Where do I intend to spend eternity after I die: heaven or hell?"*

This is your decision, my friend. No one can make it for you. It is your responsibility, not your parents' or your employer's.

Stop for a moment and take stock of your life on this planet.

You are free to do as you like. You may be living in a country where you have the right of free speech. In some countries, you are allowed to say whatever you desire, but whichever part of the world you are in, a day is coming when every man, woman and children will be held responsible and will have to give an account of their actions when they lived. Both the living and the dead will have to answer to their names on the day of judgement.

Your records will face you and all the evidence will be available. I knew of a case when the jury heard, they thought it was a waste of public money to bring the case to court. However, on the second day of the court hearing, the jury concluded and declared that the defendants were guilty as charged.

In the same manner, your case will come up before the judgement seat of God and your answer will be "Guilty as charged" because the angels keep good records.

Why not check the way you are living now? If you realise that your soul is at risk, call on God and tell him how sorry you are for the way you are living. Ask him to deliver you from sin, and tell him that you want to serve him for the rest of your life.

Time is running out. The days are shorter than we think. Satan is let loose, ready to take all those who belong to him into everlasting fire. Soon, it will be too late to do anything about it. Mercy would be gone. Talk to God *now*, because He is your only hope. He will never forsake you or let you to perish, because He is a faithful God and He loves all His creation. It is the sin they commit He hates.

If someone gave you one million pounds and tells you to tell others to come and get theirs, what would you do?

What God has done for me, I must tell others, I cannot keep it to myself. When you accept Jesus Christ as your Lord and saviour and friend, you too will be happy to tell others.

CHAPTER 12

A Living Hope

Some glad morning when this life is over, I will fly away! All my gains are only for a while. My hope is built on Jesus Christ my Lord. Hell is only fit for the devil and his angels.

There is hope beyond the grave. You will have peace and sweet rest when you surrender your life to God. Others in the past have put their trust in him and He is a faithful God who never loses a battle.

We read in the Holy Book where Gideon was going into battle with thirty-two thousand fighters, but God told him they were too many and reduced it to three hundred fighters. He won the battle.

We are also told of three men who refused to do what the king wanted them to do: serving him rather than God. They were thrown into a blazing fire, heated up seven times hotter, God sent His Son into the fire to rescue all three men.

There was another time the disciples were put in jail because they were preaching the gospel. They prayed and praised, and God sent an earthquake, blasting off the prison doors and setting His children free.

God' Son was crucified by wicked men and they put His body into a cave and sealed the cave. God sent an angel to roll away the sealed door of the cave and set His Son free.

That's the God I am talking about! Do not play with the true and living God.

Back in Jamaica, there was a man who had two shops. He managed one and his wife managed the other. He went on to another district, found a younger woman who was a nurse and got into an affair with her. They planned to invite the wife to join them for dinner in the district where his girlfriend was living. The plan was to poison the wife so that the wife would die and he would get a chance to marry this new girlfriend.

He took sick on the Thursday, died and was buried on the same Sunday they had planned to kill his wife. On the day of the man's funeral, the girlfriend confessed that was their plan.

This is a very true story. I had an accident that same day which left a scar on my foot. God will reward everyone for the deeds they have committed. It is better to fall on the rock than let the rock fall on you.

God is a loving Father. He cares for his children. He gave his only son to die for us and He promised to give eternal life if we receive Him. He is a faithful God and there is no one like our Heavenly Father. Why not give him a chance in your life?

The old song says, "If I did have wings, I would fly away..." We do not have wings now, and may be for a good reason, but the time is coming when we will be caught up and fly away to a place of rest. So we are told and so we should believe.

There is somewhere better than this troubled world and some sweet day, I will take my flight and fly away to glory land, where the angels will be waiting for me. My fare has been paid by Jesus Christ the Son of God who died for an unworthy sinner like me. In His love, He did it for me and others who are willing to acknowledge, that He did it for them too.

When He appears, I will be caught up with Him and will be with Him forevermore. I will not linger or wait.

My answer is:

"Yes Lord. I will surrender my life to you so that I will be in heaven with you and behold that mansion that you have prepared for me and all those who have given their life to you.

Help me not to wonder or fear any more. While I live on this earth, help me to do whatever you want me to do. Your will Lord and not my will be done. I wandered far away from you. Now, I am coming home to be at rest with you.

I promise never to leave you and never to stray. I acknowledge my weakness, and I surrender all to you. You have made me a promise that you will be coming back for all those who have surrendered their life to you. Help me to wait until you come again to receive all those who have committed their lives to you.

Lord Jesus, help me to do the best I can for my fellow men and women. Help me to help others in their weaknesses and find joy in doing so.

Though the winds blow, I will not fear because you are with me. You are my shepherd, you are my rock. If you do not deliver me from my enemies, I will die, Help me Lord, to be courageous in the battles of life, and on the day when my life ends on this side of life, I will be ready to accept your will and not my will!

You are the God of my salvation; you are my sole friend; you will never leave me or never forsake me.

Your love is limitless, your care is without doubt and your love is everlasting. You will never leave your beloved ones in any danger. You promised to be with all those who love you.

My Jesus, if ever I loved you, it is now. I will love you in life and I will love you in death. Help me Lord Jesus, to continue loving you in life and in death.

Son of the living God, have mercy on me. Son of the living God, help me to love all men. Son of the living God, shelter me from all unrighteousness and help me to be faithful to you. You are the God of my father. Have mercy on me. You are my source and you are my friend. Come down and deliver me from the hands of wicked men. Protect me from all danger. I surrender to you now and forever. All those who put their trust in you will never fail."

As you are standing in the shadows? You will find Jesus. Hallelujah!

I feel like shouting, dancing and skipping because Jesus loves me with an everlasting love, and if anyone should ask you who I am, tell them I am a sinner saved by grace.

I will be going home to glory where Jesus Christ has built a mansion for me. No weapon from hell can stop me from loving my God. My mind is made up to follow Him until I die, then I will take my flight to be with Him forever!

I will not surrender to the devil who is a liar and a thief, I will tell him, "Get behind me. I am heaven-bound and preparing to take my flight..."

What have I got to lose? Silver and gold cannot buy your ticket for that heavenly flight. Only the blood of Jesus Christ who died for you.

What have I to fear, leaning on the everlasting arm of Jesus Christ who died for me?

"Shine Jesus, shine in this heart of mine. When my path seems low, guide me safely home. Build a fence so that the enemy cannot overcome me. Shelter me from all evil. Hold my hands as I travel through this pilgrim land, lead me to the cross where you shed your blood to set me free.

"You have such a love for me that you were willing to leave your heavenly home to come down to this wicked world to die for me and all others who were sinners just like me.

"You are my friend, and I have made a promise that I will never leave you until the day that I shall leave this earth to my heavenly home. Then I will say goodbye world. In that mansion that you have prepared for me, I will have no rent, mortgage or household bills to pay, Your blood has paid it all. In my heavenly home, I shall be free at last, never to wonder or faint."

I am inviting you to come and join me in giving God thanks for the everlasting love that He has for me and all mankind. He loves us with an everlasting love and will protect us from all evil and danger. The first aircraft was built in 1903. My father was born 1903.

My mother told me that when I was a child, I feared the sound of planes and would go and hide myself under the bed.

I still remember one of those days when I went to hide on hearing a plane. I was about four years old and I was so scared that day! How times has changed. I have travelled on a plane so many times and do love travelling on an aircraft going to another country.

As you are reading this book, take stock of your life, say to yourself, who I am, and where do I want to spend eternity?

CHAPTER 13

We Need a Change

On the night when I gave my life to God, I went to a fare ground, I was waiting for the night to come so that I would join others at a dancing party.

However, as the night drew and I saw many people coming to the fare ground, I said to myself, "if God should come now, all would be lost." This statement must have touched the Spirit of God. I was so convicted that I did not have any more interest in dancing that night.

What will convict you to surrender your life to God? Do not wait. Tomorrow could be too late. Do what needs to be done today, because tomorrow may be too late.

The heavenly host is waiting for you to book your heavenly flight. Where you will spend eternity with God and His son Jesus Christ?

Before 1903, it would have been very difficult for people to travel back and forth. It is a great joy people of those days, seeing they now can travel to any part of the world where they could see the beauty of the world that God has created for mankind.

God has created a wonderful world for us. Unfortunately, Adam and Eve disobeyed God, and now we all suffer because of sin.

Nevertheless, there is hope. Man has been given a way of escaping the wrath of God - if we are willing to take this opportunity given to us by God. It is up to us. We must look into our lives and see where we are going.

Without God in your life, you are fit for nothing. You are just dust, getting ready to go back to the ground where you came from. A tree has more hope than what you have. A tree has its roots, so it can spring up again; but as for you and I, the only hope we have is in Jesus Christ who died for us.

Make haste while you have the privilege. Many have missed the opportunity to give their lives to God. Take it now before it is too late. Do what you need to do now. Death is certain, but life is uncertain. Whatever needs to be done today, do it.

When they ran out of wine at the wedding that Jesus and His mother went, Mary told her Son the wine had finished, but He replied her, "What does that have to do with me?" She simply told those in charge, "Whatever he says to do, do it."

The world in which we now live is very dangerous. When I was going to school as a child, I had to be in the devotion class every morning, followed by the Bible class. In the latter, we must know all the verses of Psalm 100 by heart.

"Make a joyful noise unto the Lord, all ye lands. Serve the Lord with gladness. Come before his presence with singing..."

As children, we were so happy shouting out this Psalm. If we did not know it by heart after the teacher had gone through it with us, we would get a belting. To avoid getting punished, we did our best to remember all the verses by heart.

Today, there are no Bible classes in our schools, If a Christian teacher should tell a child to go home and read the Bible, that teacher could get the sack, What a world we are living in!

If a Christian police officer should tell a fourteen-year-old boy, "Go and read your Bible", he too could get sacked. Yet, if that same boy were to commit a crime, that same police officer could be ordered to go and arrest him!

As a child, our Headteacher heard some children were making noise on the streets, so he gave all head boys and girls a notebook for them to put down the names of anyone of who made noise. One morning, a group of us children were on our way to school with the head boy. He took out the book and was about to write down some names when I warned him, 'You can't put my name down!" Of course, he put my name down and I got a caning by the headteacher.

All over the world today, the citizens are getting out of order and the authorities don't even know what to do. Our prisons are full and we do not have the money to build new prisons.

I went to Jamaica some years ago and spent a few days with a cousin who was a teacher and a Justice of the Peace. One day, she told me she did not want to see me out on the streets after 6pm. I replied, "I was born in this district. When I was a child, I could be out on the street even after twelve o'clock in the night and I would have no fear except for a ghost."

How times have changed!

Still, any nation that forgets God will feel His wrath, How can you forget God? Yet in the football ground, we sing, "God save the King!"

All nations need to get their actions right. God will deal with all who forget to serve Him faithfully. He has dealt with nations that forgot Him before, and He will again.

When I heard the news about a fourteen-year-old boy who killed a sixteen-year boy, I thought, "This is surely madness! We just cannot go on as we are." There has got to be a change in the way in which we now live. I am not academically educated, but I have seen enough in my lifetime and I have got to say something before I take my flight to glory-land.

There is something wrong with our society. How can you kill someone, and the court of law gives you a sentence of fifty years in prison, then there comes someone who claims it is against the human rights of the individual who committed the crime!

When I was young, I heard a preacher made this statement: "You cannot go to hell and act as you like, because there is order in hell!"

Today, people no longer respect the laws of the land. Some will go out full well to commit crimes and hope to get away with it. If we put them in jail and release them early, they just go and commit the crime again and then they have to go back to jail where they are given a Bible to read. When they were young, we did not give them the Bible. If a teacher had told that same boy, "Read the Bible. It says you should not kill or steal", that teacher would be putting his/her job at risk.

We need to wake up and change the way we do things! We are living in dangerous times, and the coming of Jesus Christ is very near. When He was on earth, He told us, "Look up, for your redemption draws near..."

CHAPTER 14

Hope Beyond the Grave

In Jesus Christ, there is hope beyond the grave, so seek Him before it is too late. He will be coming back as He promised in His Word: "I will be going away, but I will be coming back to receive you unto myself, so that where I am, you will be there also."

That is a very good promise given to us by our Jesus Christ, and His promises are sure.

Someone may make you a promise but fail to carry it out. In the old days, if a man wanted a woman to be his wife, he would have to give what is called a promissory note. My father broke that promise and it was something he later regretted. Do not make promises that you may not be able to fulfil.

I have no fear of Jesus coming back. My fear is that some of my relatives and friends will not be ready to take their flight to go with Him when He comes.

As someone of Jewish descendant, it was recorded that my forefathers cried out "Crucify Him and let His blood be on our children's children...."

This was a wicked statement to make, but our Lord Jesus Christ said, "Forgive them because they do not know what they have done". I am asking that you too will forgive all my ancestors foe the things they did to our Lord and Saviour.

It had to be done. Man had lost his communication with God, and the only way for Him to have that relationship restored was to send His Son to die on the cross.

There is hope, my dear friends. There is hope beyond the grave. Just repent of your sins and make a promise that you will start serving God - if you have not yet done so.

If you have accepted God, and are serving him, I encourage you to keep the fight going without looking back. Fight the cause of your faith and do not look back to where you came from or surrendering.

I am beseeching all my readers: let us take stock of the way we treat others. We only have but a few years to live together. Today we are here, tomorrow we are gone. That's a certainty.

After we have taken our flight to leave this world, that's it. Whatever the relationship we have (friends, family members, mother, brother, sister etc), we are gone, never to return again. How sad it will be that some will be in hell, burning in the fire, while some will be in heaven drinking sweet wine and honey!

I have some loving family and friends who have departed this life, and I sincerely hope I will see them again. How sad it would be seeing my dear mother and father in heaven while I am in hell or the other way round.

Stop for a while and think about it: You are on one side and your loved ones are on the other side. There will be a huge gulf between you and them. When the rich man saw Lazarus in the bosom of Father Abraham while he was in hell fire, this was what Father Abraham told him. It is a serious matter, my friend.

Please check up on the way you treat your family, friends, and even your enemies. We are told by Jesus that we should love our enemies as we love ourselves.

CHAPTER 15

Living on Borrowed Time

Make no joke about this: there won't be another world as the one we are living in now. There will be a new earth and a new heaven. This present world was not even just for birds in the air and the fish in the sea, but they do God's will while we do not.

Why would you want to stay here when there is a better place prepared for you? Look at what is happening in the world. Leaders who make mockery of people's lives. God requires that anyone who seeks to lead His people should have wisdom, that's why he added wisdom to King Solomon who asked for wisdom and not riches.

At an age like this we do not need fools leading any nation. When one fails, we all suffer. We need leaders who fear

God, do the right thing for their citizens and acknowledge that there is a God in heaven; not those who are all for themselves and their rich cats, living off the poor. They have it all while others are suffering, can't even feed their families or keep themselves warm in winter. God hates such behaviour, and He is going to do something about it in His time.

Heaven is better than this wicked world. Some people are all for themselves. Some have three or four jobs paid by taxpayers while others can't even heat their homes to keep warm.

I am just going to say it as it is, by the Spirit of the Lord that is upon me to write this book.

God has heard their cries, and He is coming down to deliver them. He has had enough of the way His people are being treated, and He is coming down with vengeance. Enough is enough. Take heed. Repent before it is too late.

What God has done to those in the past, He is ready to do now. He does not like to see His people suffer. He has acted then, and He is going to do it again. "Let my people go!"

He is coming back, not as a baby but as a King!

I am just a voice crying out in the wilderness. Nevertheless, I must say what is on my heart.

If you were told you only had six months to live, what would you do?

Several years ago, I found myself in that situation. My brother was ill and his doctor told him he had only six months to live. On hearing this, my brother stopped having any meals. One day I went to visit him, and his doctor and another person were present with us in his house. The doctor explained the situation, asking if I had anything to say.

I asked again, "How long does he have?" and she told me "Six months". On hearing the news again, I broke down in tears, knowing that the only brother that I had in the country would be leaving me soon, The doctor too broke down in tears. Not being able to save my brother from death was very sad, but that is what life is.

I lived far away from him and when the time came for me to leave, I again started to cry, knowing that he may die without having anyone with him. He was admitted to the hospital the following day, I was at the cemetery to get a burial spot prepared when l got a phone call from a doctor telling me to come to hospital immediately, because my brother was dying. Shortly after, I got a telephone call that he had died.

That's what life is. We are on borrowed time, and we have no control over events that may come our way. Therefore, seek ye the Lord while he may be found; do not wait when it may be too late.

We were put on this planet to occupy until the Lord returns. The whole world belongs to God, but some have nothing while others have it all. The day is coming when we will all have to leave everything in this world. You came here with nothing, so you will return with nothing.

Dust we are and to dust we will return to answer to our Maker. Your records will be open, and you will have to give an account of your deeds, whether it is good or bad. It does not matter how rich you are; you cannot buy yourself out of this on Judgment Day.

"Behold I come quickly, and everyone will have to give an account of the deeds done in their body..."

What will your answer be, my dear friend? Is your heart right with God? Are you washed in the blood of Jesus Christ the Son of God? Can you say, "Amen, preacher"? Are all your sins forgiven by God your Maker?

You and you alone can give an answer to these questions, your mother or your father or your bank manager cannot answer for you. They also will have to answer for themselves.

I was in America some years ago helping the farmers to harvest their crops. As the crops came in the factory, we had to get them sorted out the same day and put it in storage. One night I had to work until very late to get the green peas ready to be put in storage.

In this life we at times want things done as we want, but we believe anything concerning God must wait until you have time to do it, forgetting that our times belong to God.

You are here on earth on borrowed time. It is only lent to you my friend, and anything lent to you must be given back to the rightful owner. God is the owner of everything - including your life.

When you are dead, your body will become alive, and you will be taken to the judgement seat of God where you will have to give an account of all that you have done in your lifetime. Oh, what a day that will be!

According to the Holy Book, the saints will be judging the wicked ones, I could be one you will have to face. Be warned: I will have to judge you according to the laws of God and won't be able to deal with you lightly. If you are sinless, that will be okay with me, but if you are not, there is nothing I can do for you, but to turn you over to the angel that will be taking you to hell.

Maybe it could be your mother or father who will be your judge, or it could well be other way round. How sad that would be!

Jesus loves us so much that He gave his life for us. It does not matter who we are or what position you hold in this life - if you are a born again Christian and believe Jesus Christ His Son who died for mankind, you will be able to escape the fires of hell. If you are still living in sin, you need to repent of all sins committed. Unless you do so, there are no 'ifs', or 'buts'; you will be going to hell with the devil and his angels. If you don't believe me, get King James version of the Holy Book.

King James was once a King of England. If he could believe in the Holy Book, so should you. If he has made it into heaven, so can you, but you will have to acknowledge that Jesus died for your sins, repent, and serve the true and living God.

God loves us. I was young now I am old, yet I never seen the righteous forsaken or his seed begging bread (Psalm 37:25). He is a loving father. He does care for his children and will do anything to protect them.

He told Moses, "I have heard the cry of my people, and I come down to deliver them." Imagine God leaving His throne to deliver His people because of a wicked man.

He is ready to do the same today, my friend. Our God does not joke. He once sent a flood and wiped out a world that had rebelled against him - except Noah and his family.

He once sent a king to go and eat grass because he too was wicked and ungodly. When Gods anger turns against you, no man on earth can rescue you. Whatever you do my dear friend, do not reject your maker. Without Him, you are nothing but dust. Dust you are and to dust you shall return.

It is no joy having to be this blunt, but if a patient is very sick, the doctor will have to give some medication to get the patient better.

All nations that forget God are sick and need the blood of Jesus Christ to wash them and make them clean. You need God in your heart and soul, no matter who you are.

CHAPTER 16

When Adam Failed

God made man in His own image. He expected man to serve Him, but man disobeyed him.

God was so disappointed when He came down in the cool of the day and called Adam, but he did not answer. Just imagine having a friend you always meet at a certain time. You go to look for him but you cannot find him, and he has never done that before.

"Adam where art thou, I heard your voice, but I could not answer because I am naked."

Confession, "I heard your voice because I am naked."

"Who told you that you are naked? Have you eaten of the fruit I forbade you to eat?"

"The woman that you gave to me, gave me the fruit that you told me not to eat, and I ate it" (Genesis 3:9-12).

Here he was, blaming God! It is easy to blame others when we fail to take responsibility for our actions - which in many cases means that others suffer for the bad decisions we made.

So it was with Adam. He did not obey God and instead of repenting, he blamed both God and the woman.

Before he disobeyed, God gave him eternal life. He gave him a very beautiful woman to be his companion. Rather than agree to eat the fruit God told him not to eat, he could have rebuked his wife in love. Then when God came, he should have told Him what happened and apologised.

Maybe if he had done so, we would not be in the situation we now find ourselves in: hard labour with sweat, women having babies with hard labour and a shorter time to live.

My brother and sister, God has made a way out. Return to Him and He will give you peace in your soul and eternal life. Judgement day is coming. Run for your life before it is too late. Accept God and His promise of eternal life.

Do not wait to say, "I wish I had given my life to God," If you do not do it now, tomorrow may be too late. You would be lost, spending your time in everlasting fire. I don't want to go to hell, do you?

Hear a ninety-one year old man pleading with you to take stock of your life and decide what is best for you. I cannot make decisions for you, but if the watchman does not watch and give godly warnings, he is not fit to be a watchman.

CHAPTER 17

Let's Return to God

Parents, please let your children know there is a God in heaven, and it is their duty to love and serve him. A nation or a people that forget God is in danger.

In the Holy Book, it is said, "For God so loved the world that He gave His only son to die upon the cross" (John 3:16).

Our God is a jealous God. He says we must not have any other God than Him. There has been no other God than the one I learned about in Sunday school when I was a child. There will never be any other God.

What a mighty God we serve! He sends the summer and spring, autumn and winter. He provides food for the birds and fishes in the sea. He provides food for all animals and man - wretched souls who are doomed to die. Had it not been His mercies, we would be consumed and ready to die.

When I was a child I heard this song: *"Tell me what more can Jesus do? He feeds the hungry, heals the sick, made the blind see, cleanse the leper, raise the dead. Tell me what more can Jesus do?"*

He even promised He has gone to prepare a mansion for us. Tell me, what more can Jesus do?

The world has never had a man like Jesus living among sinners, yet He had no sin. He was full of love, but He will be coming back with vengeance to rid the world of sin.

We have gone away from God. We have done evil to God and man. We have turned away from Him, but now, you are tired of the sins you have committed and you are coming home.

My dear friend, I want to encourage you to fight the good fight and lay hold on eternal life. That is the only answer for you and I.

Life today is not easy. We, as British citizens, have gone through the second world war. I was in Jamaica then and I was only six years old, but I remember when it started and when it ended.

Our Prime Minister at the time made this comment: "We will fight them on the land. We will fight them on the sea, and we will fight them in the air. We will never surrender!"

Things have gone so bad that in this same country, which is one of the richest countries in the world, people cannot feed their children or heat their homes properly. Surely, as a nation so rich, we should be ashamed of ourselves. There are so many millionaires and billionaires, and we tax the poor.

It is a disgrace, and God is going to do something about it. Let not your heart be troubled neither let it be afraid, look up while redemption draweth near.

As humans, we are very weak. No wonder one writer wrote, "Guide me, O thou great Jehovah, I am weak but thou art mighty." Without God, we are helpless. That's why the Bible says, "He that says there is no God is a fool." It does not matter what you do with a fool; he is still a fool.

If you dress them in jeans, they are still fools. If you dress them in a suit, they are still a fool. You send them to university, they come home and are still educated fools. Why? They are only human.

The whole world is a barren land, and that's why we all need our Creator to guide us through it. After He returns to take us home to glory land, He is going to break down every structure man put up. He owns everything and He does not want anything made by man.

Both my mother and father were very kind. They would give you anything you wanted if they had it. During World War 2, I recall a woman moved to the district to live, but she could not find any where to live.

Though we did not have a large apartment, my mother gave this woman a place to stay until she could find somewhere to live. My mother put some clothes out to dry in the sun. We woke up in the morning and all the clothes were gone -including the woman. My mother did a good deed and that's what the woman repaid her with.

However, it has been said that if you do good, it will follow you, and if you do bad, it will also follow you."

As a child, I heard of an old man who always asked a woman for food. One day this woman got fed up with the old man, so she cooked some food, poisoned it and gave it to the old man. For some reason, the old man did not eat the meal this woman gave to him.

She had two sons who would always check on the old man. They told the old man they were hungry and wanted something to eat.

The old man told them he had only the food that their mother gave to him, but I did not eat it, so they could have it.

On getting home, the woman's sons told their mother that they were feeling sick. The mother asked them what they had eaten and they told her they had stopped at the old man's home and he gave them food to eat.

What she did to the old man, she did to herself. Be careful of your actions. If you do wrong, it will surely come back to you.

Let's look out for one another in love. "Greater love can no man than to give his life for his friends" (John 15:13).

In this life there are so many problems, and sometimes you feel like giving up, but my encouragement to you is this: don't give up; there is hope. Our Lord Jesus Christ also felt like giving up when He was in the garden praying, but He came down to earth to do His father's will.

We are told He got on His knees and prayed, "Father, if it is possible, let this cup pass from me, nevertheless, not my will but yours" (Matthew 26:39).

It was a bitter cup, and no one should have to go through such a agony, but there was a job to be done.

CHAPTER 18

We Need Jesus!

I am of a mixed race, part European, part Jewish, and part African.

I was born in the Caribbean. I migrated to the United Kingdom at age 23, going on 24. My intention was to work for five years and then return to my place of birth. However, I have been in the U.K for over sixty years, and as things are, I have no intention to return to my place of birth.

I came to drink the milk and not count the cows, but my children and grandchildren are here to drink the milk and own the cow.

I came to work for someone and get paid, but one of my sons chose to work for himself and he is doing very well, along with his beautiful English wife. We have two beautiful mixed-race grandchildren and great-grandchildren. We have other great-grandchildren, and we love them all dearly.

I give praise to God for all that He has done for me. I put my trust in Him, and what He has done for me and many others, He will do for you. I am encouraging you to put your trust in the true and living God. He is the best friend you could ever have. Put your trust in Him and at the end of day, you will be able to get on the heavenly plane and take your flight to the heavenly home.

If you are down, put your trust in God. If you are fearful, put your trust in Him. If everything seems impossible, put your trust in God. I once was lost, but Jesus found me. I once was wandering, but God saved me.

Before Adam failed God, we were meant to live forever, but because of his disobedience, you and I have been robbed of thousands of years. Life in this present world has been difficult, as man cannot even rule himself, let alone rule others.

What we need in today's world is godly men and women who fear God so much that they seek to have wisdom to lead God's children in a better way than we see in today's society.

My wife and I have six wonderful children. If it was in today's world, I am not sure I would have one or two at the most. Parents should know best how to take care of their children and not allow the Government, or anyone else, to tell them how to bring up their children. Why should others be telling my children who they are, when in fact they were born as God wanted them to be?

Let us all who have reasonably good wisdom, bring up our children in a God-fearing manner.

Great Britain is a very good country. I have lived in two cities in this country and travelled to many other parts of the country. I have also lived in two other countries and travelled to many countries. The world is a beautiful place to be in, but mankind has made a mockery of God's wonderful world.

Look at what is happening to the world today. Right now, we have three or more wars, and unless God intervenes, we will soon see a third world war. Can we afford another world war? We do not want to have another war, but there will be one before I leave this world, and it will be more serious than the last world war.

We need to seek God before it is too late. He alone can protect us from all dangers.

Where would you prefer to be: heaven or earth? Make your choice. I'd rather love to be with Jesus than anywhere else. Heaven is a better place to be: no sickness, no war, everlasting life and all things that I would ever want are free. Give me Jesus all the time!

Each and everyone needs to have Jesus Christ in our lives. I recommend him to you. So many others over the ages have put their faith in him and He never failed anyone. Our days are in his hands. He is an everlasting Father to all His children from generations to generations. His promises are for everyone. What He says, He will do.

What better confidence can you have, knowing that whatever part of the world you go, He will be there to protect you? He promised never to leave you alone,

What better power do you need? If you are sick, He will heal you in His time. If you are hungry, He will feed you, If you cannot pay your bills, He will make a way for you. If you are put into a fire, He will send His Son into the fire with you. If you are sent to jail wrongfully, He will send an earthquake to blast the prison door down and set you free.

All these events are recorded in His holy book. Do not wait any longer. Do it now.

CHAPTER 19

Be Encouraged: God is Faithful

Are you downhearted? Don't give up. Are you lonely? Don't give up. Does it seem impossible? Don't give up. You cannot pay your bills? Do not worry, God will make a way out for you.

Some years ago, my wife was ill and I was due to pay a debt. I was in church on the Sunday but all that was on my mind was that debt due to be paid on Monday. While I was still worrying about how I would get the money, someone gave me a note wrapped up. When I opened it, there was money in the note, sent to me from the Pastor. "The Lord laid it on my heart to give you this money," he wrote in the note. Please do not tell anyone that I gave you this money." As the song goes, "Why worry when you can pray?"

My wife and I have often emptied our bank account and given money to the church to help pay the mortgage on the church.

Over thirty years ago, things were not very good for us financially. I went on a ten-day fast. One of those days, I lay down on my back, shut my eyes, stopped my breath and prayed to God, telling Him, "If you can't help me, take my life now."

Since that day, things have been much better with us financially. We have been able to pay all our debts when due.

All my life, God has been good to me. I encourage you to put your trust in Him and He will surely help you.

A prophet named Elijah was lonely and depressed. Queen Jezebel wanted to kill him, so he went away and hid himself under a broom tree. This tree had a rounded shape and is not found in Europe or the United Kingdom. However, because of its shape, it could provide shade to someone lying down.

This prophet had once called down fire from heaven so that the people could know the true God, but at this point, he was very lonely and at the same time, had nothing to eat, so he prayed that God would take his life (the same prayer I also once prayed!).

God sent an angel to encourage him and sent a crow to feed him. We have crows in the West Indies. They eat dead meat, so no way would I want to eat from a crow, but if God said so, it had to be done.

My dear reader, be encouraged, knowing that there is one who will help you when you are in need.

When my wife was expecting our fifth child, our doctor sent her to the hospital to see a consultant. Upon examination, he told her that she should agree to having an abortion because there would be complications if she decided to give birth. My wife told the Consultant that we would not agree to abort the baby because we are Christians.

When the time came for her to give birth, I phoned the hospital to tell them my wife was in labour and they told me to get an ambulance to bring her to the hospital while they got the theatre ready as agreed earlier. Upon reaching the hospital, she gave birth within ten minutes without any complications. That child has grown to be a healthy adult today, working in the health service as a manager.

What a mighty God we serve! He is good in the morning, He is good in the daytime and He is good in the night. He is just good all the time.

All the days of my life, He has been good to me and by His grace, I will serve and trust him until the day I die.

Joshua told the Israelites, "Choose ye whom you will serve: if the living God, serve him, if any other God. Decide whom you will serve"(Joshua 24:15).

If God had not been with me, what would have happened to me?

Chapter 20

The Best Decision I ever Made

Come and let's reason together. There is a living God, whether you believe it or not, so be wise and start believing now if you have not done so.

From a very young age, I learned that there is a God, and I did believe then, and I believe even now. I was brought up to love God, and his Son Jesus Christ, from a very young age. Other children and I used to go home from church, singing, "Yes, Jesus loves me, for the bible tells me so."

Oh, those childhood days! Some young men loved to hear us sing and would pay us to sing again. We were glad to sing again to be paid!

I have been in ill health for over six years. The pains in my body these years is beyond describing in a way you can understand, I have been admitted to hospital several times. I have seen so many doctors, and had many tests, all will be successful, yet the pains continue.

I have even spent a lot of money getting private treatment, to no avail. Nevertheless, our God can do what is to be done in His own time. Never will I give up on God, I will trust Him now, and I will trust Him until the day I die. He is my father and friend,

I lost my parents a long time ago, and I hope to meet them when I get over on the other side, yet even if they were alive, I would have to trust God. He is God and he cannot lie. He stands by His words: "Come unto me and I will give you life."

On one of my many visits to the hospital, I told a doctor, "It is better if I die." But she replied, "Do not say that." That was how I felt at the time. Nevertheless, I give God thanks that I am alive and now writing this book to encourage all to put their trust in God our creator.

Many years ago, I saw a man who was born the same year as I was, but he was looking twenty or even thirty years older than me.

Again, some twenty or thirty years ago, I went to a funeral and when we got to the cemetery, near the grave where this person's grave was, there was a headstone. I started reading what was written on this headstone, and realised the person that was buried there was born the same year I was born.

I give God thanks for sparing by life to see this day, and by His grace, I hope to see many more years. There is hope beyond the grave, so while it is day, do the best you can to others. We will not be here for ever.

I grew up with some other young people and lately I heard that they have all died. I felt very sad getting the news, but that's what life is all about: here today, gone tomorrow, I may not see them again, but God knows everything. He controls our lives.

May I encourage you to be at peace with others, even your enemies? Soon this life will all be over. The person you see today, you may never see again. I beseech all young people as a father: love and respect your parents and all others.

The way you respect others today will come back to you later in life. We might not all get on together. We may have some ways too hard for others to accept. Try to meet each other halfway.

While working on the buses, a young woman told me she would love having me as her husband. I asked her, "How do you know if we would get on?" and she responded, "If your wife can put up with you, so can I".

"See me" and "Live with me" are two different things. Jamaicans also have a saying: "Do not buy a puss in the bag!"

It takes a lot to be satisfied in this life, but we will be satisfied when we get to heaven. The hope of having a better life is far outstanding, and I won't look back. The joy of knowing that when I die, my soul will go back to God makes me feel like dancing, skipping, shouting and praising my God!

What better decision could I have taken than to accept Jesus Christ as my personal saviour? Now, I am on my way to take my flight to that heavenly home. It gives me great joy to invite you to give your life to God. He will make you a different person. Places you used to go, you will go there no more, words you used, you will use them no more.

Am I trying to force religion on you? No. I am not trying to do that, but if it were possible, I would get another minister and a Christian doctor, hold you down and inject the blood of Jesus Christ into your body! That would be the best injection you could ever get in your life.

There is no better time to seek God than now, because tomorrow may be too late.

The devil is a liar. He comes to kill and destroy. His plan is to take people into everlasting fire. Have you ever got burnt by fire? Hell fire will be worse.

A day is coming when all those who did not give their life to God will be lost in the pit of hell and neither God, Jesus Christ or I would like to see you in hell.

There are going to be millionaires and billionaires in hell, but they won't be able to help anyone because they would be broke and helpless themselves. They don't need money. They need release from hell, and the devil can't release them, because Jesus has the key for hell.

The rich man died and went to hell. When he saw Lazarus in the arms of Abraham, he begged Abraham to send him to dip his finger in the water to assuage his thirst. Abraham told him there was a gulf between them both, so that could not happen. Very sad story, but that is what is going to happen to anyone who does not give their lives to God.

This is why I am asking you to surrender your life to God before it is too late. What would it profit you to gain the whole world and lose your soul? You can't say nobody shared the gospel with you. As a believer, I cannot do otherwise, because we have a duty to spread the gospel and to tell others the good news that Jesus Christ gave His life for you and me.

There are two roads to choose: heaven or hell. One is wide and the other is narrow. Which road are you going to choose? Choose this day who you will serve: God or the devil.

One song writer wrote, "I would rather have Jesus than any other thing." Not too long ago a billionaire drowned in the sea, I felt sad to hear of such a death, but that's life.

Earnestly and tenderly, Jesus is calling you home. The Holy Ghost is telling you to return home! The prodigal son, who found himself eating pig food said, "I am going back home to my father's home..."

Will you arise and go home? Will you arise and tell Jesus you are coming home to be with Him until the day you die? He is waiting for your return to Him. Do not put it off for tomorrow, because; tomorrow may be too late. Do it now!

Yes, the prodigal son returned home, glad that his father was willing to welcome him home. It will be a great joy to hear that someone has come home to God and His Son. I made that decision over seventy years ago and I am glad. Nobody told me the road would be easy, but I glad I am not counting the costs. Life has been very difficult at times, but God is over me and is keeping me alive. I made one of the best decisions in my life.

Where could I go but to the Lord? He has rescued me from the devil and hell. He saved my soul, washed me in the blood of His son and set me free. My life was changed. The lifeboat rescued me, I am now free from all sin, getting ready for my flight to my heavenly home.

Jesus has made a promise to be with me all the days of my life. What better friend could I have? He walks with me, and He tells me I am His own.

Jesus said, "I will be with you forever; I will never leave you nor forsake you. I will be with you in life, and I will be with you in death, and at the end of death, I will give you eternal life".

You can take Him at His word, because He keeps His promises.

When you are unhappy, peace be still. When everything seems dark, peace be still. When nothing seems to be going well, peace be still. When your heart is broken, peace be still. When your friends forsake you, peace be still. When the sea storms blow hard, peace be still.

What a precious friend!

If I am low in my spirit, He will be there to say, "Fear not, I will be with you in life and in death. Be courageous, I am God and I change not. There is no other God than me. I will be in the fire with you".

"Fear not, I made heaven and the whole world. I put the sun in the sky, I made all things and there is no other God besides me. I will comfort you all the days of your life. All those who put their trust in me will never have any fear. I have done it before and I will do it again. I will deliver all those who put their faith in me."

"I have delivered all those who put their trust in me. Surely, I will do it again."

"I am Jehovah God. When I shut one door, no man can open it, and when I open one door, no man can close it. Be not afraid, I am with you to the end, so says God."

CHAPTER 21

A Guarantee and A Promise

When we walk with the Lord and do what He says, there is no other way than to trust and obey,

There is no good complaining that you have been dealt with severely. In life, there are rules that you must obey. At a traffic light, if the red light is showing, whether you are a driver or pedestrian, you must stop, otherwise, someone is going to get injured or even killed.

Whoever is in the wrong will have to answer many questions. The police will get involved, as well as the ambulance service. The local authorities, the courts and an insurance company have to get involved. You see, one person made an error, and a lot of people get involved.

So did Adam the first man God made. He disobeyed God and we all must suffer severely. However, one Man was crucified, to save millions. God is a God of love. "You killed my son, because I sent Him down to earth, but I forgive you if you repent of your sins."

You do me one 'bad', but I do you more than one 'good'. I washed you in my Son's blood that you may have everlasting life and a mansion in my heavenly kingdom, You have my guarantee: to protect you all the days of your life. I have given my son to die upon that cruel cross so that you may be saved. Tell me what more my Son and I could do? I promised to protect you all the days of your life. I have opened up the windows of heaven so that you will have everlasting life. Tell us what more can we do,.."

What better things can be bestowed on a wretched sinner like you and I?

Seek ye the Kingdom of God before it is too late.

Chapter 22

A Promise of Rest

Jesus said, "I have given my life for you." What have you given to Him?

Tell me what more Jesus can do. He has opened the windows of heaven, ready to take you in. You only have to say yes and make up your mind to give Jesus a chance in your life.

Stop waiting for a set time to surrender your life to God.

Recently, I read an article that a husband got up late in the night after he received a phone call telling him a car he was interested in had arrived. He did not tell his wife where he was going because he wanted to give her a surprise. After waiting in the night to hear from him, she started getting concerned. After waiting for his phone call, a call came from a doctor telling her to come to the hospital urgently.

On arrival at the hospital, she saw a doctor who told her what happened: he had an accident and was rushed to the hospital, but he did not make it.

This man wanted to buy a car for his wife. He did not leave his home to have an affair as many men do. But, because he is a man who is also subject to evil, death knocked at his door when he did not expect it.

This reminds me of a story I heard some years ago. A church bishop was having an affair with a church member. After the girlfriend and the wife got into a fight in the church, the girlfriend obviously felt ashamed and migrated to America. The bishop went to visit this girlfriend and he had a heart attack and died. His wife had to go to America to bring back her husband's body.

To all Christians: let your light shine so that others will see the light of salvation in you and give themselves to God.

That Bishop allowed the devil to come into his life at a time when he took his eyes off Jesus.

As a licensed minister, I am not going to take sides with this Bishop. What he allowed the devil to do was wrong, and it was a great pity he allowed the devil to lure him to go to America to see this woman. Be warned: the axe is waiting to cut you down if you fail to shine the light. Always let your light shine, my sisters and brothers.

My advice to everyone is this: do not be angry when anyone fails you. We are humans and we all can fail if we take our eyes off Jesus.

Peter in the Bible failed God so many times, but when he received the Holy Ghost on the day of Pentecost, he preached and thousands of people got saved. He also told the crippled man, “Silver and gold we do not have, but in the name of Jesus Christ rise and walk.”

Some years ago, I visited Israel, and I saw the temple and doorway where this crippled man was always sitting, waiting to get alms from all who came in and out of the temple.

There is good in all of us. It is just the devil, a thief of all things, who makes man to sin. Thank God Jesus made a way when He went on that cross and paid the ultimate price by shedding His blood. It was a heavy price, but He paid it.

When I think about Jesus, and what He has done for me, my soul cries out, “Hallelujah! Thank God, He has saved me”.

I was lost and undone, but He rescued me from sin. Had he not come into my soul on that day seventy years and more ago, I do not know what would have happened to me. He calls out to anyone who would listen, “Come, ye that are weary and loaded heavily. Come, and I will give you rest for your soul. My yoke is easy, and my burden is light. Come away and I will give you rest.”

All those who are waiting, I am waiting to come into your hearts. I am knocking at the door of your hearts, waiting for you to open your door; waiting for you to decide who you will serve.

Please do not miss this opportunity. You only have one life. Come and find rest and peace for your soul. Bring everyone you know - including your family. Make hay while the sun shines. The earlier you do it, the sweeter it will be, the heavenly host is waiting to receive you.

Joy awaits you when you return to God. When you receive him, your seat on the heavenly plane will be booked for you, ready to take your flight to that mansion Jesus has gone to prepare.

CHAPTER 23

Settle Your Accounts Now

I was taking a walk one day and I decided to visit a cemetery where some relatives were buried. As I looked at the headstones, my heart trembled. I saw the ages of those who passed on, and realised how lucky I was to be alive.

A day will come when others will say the same thing when they think about us!

You are alive only by the mercies of God, and He is waiting for you to decide who you will serve. Those waiting in their grave may have settled their accounts a long time ago waiting to receive their rewards. Settle yours while you are alive, so you can know where you are going.

As a religious man and a licensed minister, I have great concern for the souls of men. Hell is certain, and so is heaven. God made man to worship and honour Him all the days of his life. According to the Bible, we were not created to die. Had Adam not sinned, it was God desire that we should live forever.

If you were promised five million pounds not to do certain things, and you did it, would you still expect to receive the five million pounds?

Adam was told clearly, "The day you eat the fruit from that tree, you will die". I do not know what language God spoke in that age, but this man's disobedience costs us eternal life and hard labour for women giving birth to children.

We live in a world that is full of trouble, but there is a better place where there will be no more sickness and no more death. He who has this hope, purifies his or her heart. There is a better place waiting for you and I on the other side.

This hope is built on solid ground, and I have no reason to fret or be dismayed.

"For God so loved the world that he gave his only son to die for us all."

I have three sons, and I am not too sure if I would want to let any one of them make that sacrifice. Knowing them as well, I do not think they would be willing to give their lives for mankind. Both myself and them are only human. We do not mind doing some things for ourselves, but to do those things for others is a problem.

I recall a book I read as a child of a man called Brother Anancy. He went to the market and bought five plantains.

Having cooked the plantains, he gave one each to his four children and one to his wife. He then started moaning that he did not get any, so they each gave him half of theirs. He got more than what they got!

Clever? No. Why didn't he buy six plantains in the first place? Maybe he did not have any more cash. If it was in our days, he would have used his credit card - if he was credit worthy.

Mr. Macmillan - the prime minister when I first came to England - made this statement: "The nation never had it so good!" For the first time, we got a large sum of tax rebate as never before.

Do not be a selfish person. The more you give, the more you get. Give God a chance in your life, and when you have done so, tell others of the new life you are now living. Just pass it on. A holy living is worth living.

CHAPTER 24

Seek God First

I am sure you are not comfortable with the way you are now living, - rich or poor. If you are millionaire, you want to be billionaire. If you are poor, you want to get rich.

My plan was to be a millionaire by age thirty-five. Am I a millionaire now? I am not, even at 90 plus! "Why aren't you?" you may ask. It is because I am a man and men sometimes fail. Maybe God did not want me to be a millionaire because if I was that wealthy, I might not have given my soul to Him.

"Seek ye the kingdom of God first, and all other things will be given to you." Whatever is for you will be given to you. When you accept God in your life, everything will change. Maybe if you were to do the lottery and win, then you would become rich.

In this life, there are things you should not do, even when your life could be more comfortable.

I experienced a great change after I gave my life to God. I am heaven-bound and I leave worldly things alone. Having Jesus Christ in your life is profitable. You are losing nothing. Your loss is heaven's gain and you will receive eternal life which is far better than silver and gold.

A man once lived in Port Royal, the capital town of Jamaica. This city was full of rich people. My father told me the Spanish and Europeans would go overseas, steal gold from other countries and bring the gold back to Jamaica. The man and most of the people living in this capital city were very rich and forgot God.

There was an earthquake and one of the wicked men in the city was involved. It was said that the earth took him in twice. The third time it took him down, he was never seen again.

Do not play with God. His eyes are watching over every step we take in this world. The whole earth belongs to him, and He will not spare us if we forsake him and do as we like.

It is better to obey His commands, and seek to do what God wants you to do. You cannot hide from God, even if you take the wings of the birds and fly away, or you go and hide in the deepest part of the sea. His eyes are watching you.

Your best choice is to surrender your life to him and get ready to take your flight on that heavenly journey and reap the heavenly rewards waiting for you.

It gets sweeter every day. Get on board! Heaven is better than this!

I am writing this book with great joy and I can feel the Holy Spirit of God upon me. I am convinced that God is pleased with me and I am happy to share what He has done for me.

I am not very educated, but I will use what I have. When God appeared to Moses to go and tell Pharaoh to let His people go, Moses did not want to go. He gave many excuses. He had a rod, and God asked him, "What is in your hands?" He told him to use it.

Because Moses stretched out the rod, the Red Sea was divided, and the Israelites could cross the Red Sea on dry ground, He again stretched out the rod again, all Pharaoh's army drowned.

Use what is in your hand. Do not sit idle and let the enemy get the better of you.

Fight the good fight of faith. You have a duty to fight for your family and your friends. Fight with all your might and do not give up. Fight until your enemies are dead or no longer able to fight.

Do not allow the devil to get away with your family. Some may go astray, but keep fighting. The battle is not yours, but God's!

Caleb in the Bible said, "I am now eighty years old; I am as strong as I was forty years ago and I am willing to fight."

In God's army, you do not stop fighting. We had a song that went this way:

"I will fight until I die. I will never run away..."

Stand up and fight the old dragon! Satan will never stop discouraging God's people. When I was a young Christian, we were told Satan met up with Evangelist Moody just after he finished preaching in the service. He brought to attention all the bad things that Moody had done before he got saved. Moody accepted that he had done them all, but the blood of Jesus Christ had covered them all.

Do not allow Satan to discourage you. We were told Satan was selling his tools. He had an old one which he failed to get rid of, and when asked why he was not getting rid of this old rusty tool, he replied that was the one he used to discourage the Christians. It was that old tool of discouragement. It is very easy to be discouraged by others.

Through faith, you can do anything you want to do. Have faith that you can move mountains. You have the authority to say, "In the name of Jesus, mountain, Go!"

CHAPTER 25

Jesus: A Friend Like No Other

I have a friend who walks with me, He talks with me, and He tells me I am His own. His name is Jesus the son of God, and He can be your friend too. When I am lonely, He says, "Cheer up. I am with you and my promise never to leave you remains forevermore."

What better friend could I have than one who has given His life for me? He called me His friend, and I recommend Him to you. Make Him your friend too. He can meet your every need. He told us in the Holy Book, "Fret not for tomorrow."

I mentioned earlier in this book that He has made ways for me which seemed impossible, but that's who He is: a provider for all our needs. Just take Him at His word.

All other friends might fail, but you can tell Him everything, and He will tell it to no one but His father because they are three in one: Father, Son and Holy Ghost. What better joy could one have, knowing there is a friend you can depend on when life gets tough, and you do not have to worry because He cares for you?

While writing this book, the Pope, who is one of the highest orders in Christianity, gave his Easter blessings on a Sunday and died on Monday. Death does not have any respect for anyone. When your time comes, that is it!

One of the stories we were told as children was that when someone feels death is coming, they would get up and make attempts to run. Death would not have any of this nonsense, so when it is time for a man to die, he hits him on the feet first, so that he cannot walk. Yes, it is just a story, but when death arrives, you had better make sure it is well with your soul. That's all God wants to know. Is it well with your soul?

He is coming soon. Don't tarry any longer, seek Him now while you have the chance.

CHAPTER 26

Keep Your Eyes on Jesus

If heaven was not my home, dear Lord, what would I do?

I am tired of this world and its troubles. I mentioned in one of my earlier books that my mother told me she was in labour for three days before she had me. When she told me this as a young child, my response was, "Maybe I did not want to come into this wicked world!"

I have seen enough and heard enough to show how wicked humans can be, and how the human heart can conceive all the evil that goes on daily over the world. Where is the love we should have for one another?

You are here for no more than seventy years. If you are blessed like me, you may live beyond ninety. Still, it does not matter who you are, or how rich you are; you will have to leave everything you have on this earth behind.

Your loved ones may bury you in the best suit or dress, but you won't even know what you are buried in.

My mother told me that when I was a child, I used to see a lot of 'duppy' or what we know as ghosts. When I was about twelve years old, I was outside and saw a figure that looked like a ghost. When I told my mother what I saw in the night, she told me she heard some knocking on the window. According to popular belief, if you see a ghost, they will come and listen if you are telling someone about it and they may harm you.

Why do you want to know if I am telling someone what I saw? It is dead, and should stay in the grave until the day of judgement.

The dead do not have anything to do with the living, but the dead do know what goes on in the world they were once living in.

On my father's side, there is a family burial ground. At about the age of 13-14 years old, my brother and I went up to this big land as we called it and my brother did something wrong. During the night our grandfather told our father in a dream what my brother had done, and he told our father to tell my brother that he should not do what he did again.

My brother wanted to deny it, but our father insisted. He said, "Yes, you did something wrong because my father told me in a dream." It was then that I told him what my brother had done.

Endeavour to do all the good you can, so that after you have departed this life, you can leave behind an everlasting mark. Let's be like Jesus, who after over two thousand years, He is still remembered for all the good He did on earth.

The good you do will follow you throughout generations to come. Always sow good seeds. Do not leave any iniquities that will follow your children's children.

As the day dawns and the shadow falls away, if you keep your eyes on Jesus the son of God, your shadows will fade away. Yes, life is very hard, more so for the poor, but there is a God in heaven who is looking down on everything that man does on earth, and when He has had enough, He will come down from heaven and deliver His people.

He did it for the Israelites and He will do it for you. He says, "Just stand still and know that I am God." He has never lost a battle. What He says He will do, He will do it.

Hear ye the word of the Lord:

"I am God, and I change not," thus sayeth the everlasting God.

"Lift your faith, my people. What I say I will do, I will do it. Just stand still and see my salvation towards the children of men. I cannot and will not change. Come unto me, and no longer tarry. Come now and I will give you rest.

"I am your Heavenly Father, and I am waiting for you to come home unto me, you have wandered far away from me, but I am waiting for you to come home and take your rest. You have waited far too long. Come home now while it is day. Tomorrow may be too late.

"My heavenly host is waiting to welcome you home. Come, and take your rest from your labour. My yoke is easy and my burden is light.

"Because of your soul, I sent my only Son to die for you and He was crucified by wicked men, but it was because of my love for you that I sent Him. He will be coming back to take His chosen ones home. Will you accept my invitation and come home?

"Adam, the first man I created disobeyed, and you were all doomed for hell, which was only made for the devil because he too rebelled against me. For this cause, I turned against man. But in my love, I sent my Son to die for the man, rich and poor. My salvation is not up for sale; my love is free to all mankind. The blood of my Son has paid for the ransom of your soul. Just heed the call and come home to me your everlasting father.

"Some day, my Son will be coming back and only those who accept the calling to come home will be able to take their heavenly flight to the mansion awaiting them.

"What will your answer be? You won't be able to say no one told you there was a living God and you should worship Him with all your heart. My servant is now telling you to return to your Maker. Come home, my child. I am here ready to receive you. Come home while it is day."

Chapter 27

There's No Greater Love

Having served God from my late teens, every day gets better. Having the Holy Spirit of God as your guide in life is imperative. You just cannot afford not having the Him to guide you.

The enemy of our souls, who is the devil, only comes to steal our joy and our souls. He does not care who you are. He will go into any palace or prison, or even the place where a man is dying at home or in the hospital or prison and tell him there is no God. He knew Job was serving the true God, and he asked God for permission to touch him. Despite his challenges, Job's response was, "Even though he slays me, yet I will trust him."

Greater love no man has than to give His life upon a cross so that we can live. Oh what love!

I am here to give you this good news: there is a God who loves you. Are you willing to leave your wicked ways and return to God?

You can say,

"I have wandered far away from God, now I am coming home. I have walked away from God, now I am coming home. I have wasted many days and I am feeling very lonely. Now, I am coming home.

"Oh God, I am sorry for my sins but I am coming home to be with you my God and my redeemer Jesus Christ who died for me upon that cross.

"Help me my heavenly father, to turn away from my wicked ways, and to follow you all the remaining days of my life so I can live forever and reign with you in the heavenly home. Shelter me from the gates of hell. Help me to live a holy life now and forever. You are the shelter in the time of storm.

"You have put a rainbow in the sky to remind me that You will never send a flood again to destroy the world, but only those who accept You and Your Son will escape the wrath You have planned for all those who rejected You.

"Heavenly Father, please give me the faith to live a sinless life for the remaining days of my life here on earth. Give me the faith to love and trust You. I have made a promise to serve You until I depart this life. Because of your love, I can face tomorrow. I am only human, and I am liable to fall, but guide me in my weakness, because Your ways or not my ways,

"I have heard of all the things You have done in the past for all those who put their trust in You. I have heard how you sent your Son into the fire to deliver three men from the fire. I have heard how you sent an earthquake to blast open a prison door. I have heard there is nothing impossible for you.

"Lord Jesus, I am coming home to be with you and your father forever. Blessed assurance, you are mine this day and unto eternity. What a blessed hope for all those who believe in You.

"My hope is built on nothing less than Jesus Christ who died for all mankind. It is so sweet to trust in Him!"

CHAPTER 28

Some Help for Your Christian Journey

I am now going to lead you into the good wine, meant for the last. When I started writing this book, I depended on God to lead me because I desire that all who read it should surrender their lives to God.

All through my life, I wanted to leave something behind for others to know there is a true God, and He should be glorified and given the praise. I have looked up some scriptures to help guide you to put your faith in the Lord God of heaven.

To get a licence to drive on the highways and motorways in the United Kingdom, you need to know the highway code. Without it, you would be in great danger to others and yourself.

When I was working on the London transport buses, they were trying out how best the system could work by having one-man bus operations. We were going into Central London where the first lane was for buses only. A motorist went into the bus lane and our bus collided with this other vehicle. Upon giving our report of what had happened, our manager told us they would be fighting the matter.

You see, before then, it would have been okay for any motorist to drive on that lane, but things had now changed.

So, it is with all those who decide to follow the ways of the righteous. It will bring a great change in your life.

A story was told to us when I was still a young Christian: A church member went to a place where a child of God was not expected to be. Unfortunately, death came and she died. Two angels came, one for the devil and one for God, each pointing out their claim for this individual. In the end the devil's angel said to the heavenly angel, "She is on my ground. She should not be here, therefore, I am claiming her for myself."

Those days, we shunned whatever looked like sin (even when it was not).

When I was young, I just loved reading the word of the Lord. Some years ago, I took time to read whole Bible and I was truly blessed doing so. I did not write it. Men who were inspired by God did, and it is your rule book to a better life. Hence, I have chosen the following scriptures for you to read. They will help you on your Christian journey.

- Romans 3:9-26
- Isaiah 55:7
- Acts 16:31
- Acts 3:3
- Ezra 1:2
- 2 Kings 14:25
- Matthew 12
- Psalms 140:4
- Isaiah 45:12
- Psalms 10:12
- Psalms 34
- Psalms 86
- Jeremiah 33
- Romans 10:13
- Isaiah 58:9
- Zechariah 15:9

- Romans 10:13
- 2 Timothy 2:22
- Psalms 56:16
- Psalms 1
- Psalms 14:1
- Psalms 122

Sometimes, you feel lonely and no one seems to care. You have done all that you thought was right but things are low. I have felt like that at times, and it is because we are humans and this flesh is very weak.

When Jesus was approaching the time when He was to be crucified, He prayed to His father, "If it is possible, let this cup pass from me..."

This was when He was on 'mummy's side', but when He got back to His daddy, He said, "Not my will but your will be done."

You see, when we are on 'mama's side', we become weak and lonely. We do not want to face what we are going through.

Peter told the crippled man, "In the name of Jesus Christ, rise up and walk!" When we are in the Lord, we can move mountains, but when the flesh gets weak, we are little babies wanting milk when we should be eating hard food.

Yes, our mother's love is always there. When I was a child, if you touched me, my mother would do you harm if she got you. An older boy once hit me on the nose. When I got home and my mother saw the blood on my face, she went to the home where the boy was having his lunch break. As a crowd gathered, they had to hold her, otherwise some serious things would have happened that day!

Here are a few more scripture passages you can read:

- Exodus 3:8
- Psalms 95
- Psalm 100
- Psalm 23

Our Heavenly Father is our shepherd. Let Him lead you to green pastures, and restore your soul. You may walk through the valley of the shadow of death, but will fear no evil, because He is with you all days of your life.

CHAPTER 29

Consider Your Ways

We now live in a world where it seems everyone is self-centred.

"I have a meal and somewhere to live. Those who do not have the basics have brought it on themselves..."

We are our brothers and sisters in accordance with God's plan, and we should take care of one another.

When I was a child, my great-grandmother cooked enough food to last the following day. Anytime you visited her in the day, she always had a meal to give to you. Where have all that love for others gone?

We need to go back, look at ourselves and return to our creator, Jehovah God Almighty. It is He who has made us; we did not make ourselves. All nations have turned away from God, and we need to get back to Him, because that is the only way, my friends. We found ourselves in this predicament because the first man disobeyed God, but He has given us hope by sending His son to die on the cross.

What are you going to do about the situation we are now in?

From my point of thinking, there are plenty in the world who can feed, clothe and give shelter to everyone in the world, but why do some people have so much, while others can't feed, clothe and shelter their family in a reasonable manner?

Why should one man have billions while others do not have a pound, shilling or pence in their pocket? God is the Father of all mankind and He cares for the poor. Jesus said, "It is easier for camel to go through a needle, than a rich man go to heaven."

It is pointless to have billions in your bank account and you cannot take any of it. The solution to these is that man should accept that his way is contrary to God's way of God, repent of all sins committed, and return to his former state by having a good relationship with our Heavenly Father.

I beseech you: consider your ways and acknowledge that you have sinned, but now you are coming home to Him, never no more to roam. A sinful lifestyle is no good for anyone. Rather, it is the whole duty of man to serve God and keep His commandments.

You did not make yourself. You were made in His image. You just cannot go on in life like that. There is no other way to be redeemed back to God, but by acknowledging that you are a sinner, doomed to die. Because Jesus gave His blood upon that cross, you have a hope,.Why not accept it now and return to God before it is too late?

Yes, I am a licensed Minister of the gospel, but I take no pride to have such a license. It was bestowed unto me, because my church saw it fit to give me this opportunity wherewith, I can help others to find a way to return to God.

I do not know how many more years I will be alive on this earth, but whatever the cost, I just want to make it into heaven, because I have been warned. If I fail to serve God righteously, I will be going to hell, and I do not want to go to hell when I depart this life.

If it was in this life only I had hope, I would be a man most miserable. Life is so hard and there is no way I want to go to hell - when there is hope beyond the grave.

When the trumpet sounds in the last day, I want to be on that heavenly flight to be with Jesus and His Father and all those who have been redeemed. What about you?

This is a friendly but firm warning. Be wise, take stock of your life, where do you want to be after you die: heaven or hell? The choice is yours. A day is coming when everyone will have to give an account of what they have done while living on earth. No one will be able to get away with wrong-doing, regardless of who they are. You will not be able to get away with any wrongs you have done.

It is a very foolish thing for anyone to go through a red traffic light; you are putting others at risk during so. Likewise, going through life without having God to direct your path is dangerous. So, seek ye the way wherewith it will be well with your soul.

CHAPTER 30

The Choice of a Lifetime

Life is going to be better, my friends. There is hope and anyone who has this hope in him purifies himself or herself. Our Heavenly Father has given us a way of escape from hell fire. Why not take it while you can? I was given the chance to seek a better earthly living by migrating to the United Kingdom and I took it.

I have mentioned that my mother's father was a Jew. That it makes me wonder if any of my ancestors were the ones who said to "crucify him and let His blood be on our children's children."

How foolish it was to make a comment like that, pronouncing an evil on your generation to come, but we are man, and we do and say foolish things. Out of all the things God made, man is the only one He regretted making. If it wasn't for His love, we all would perish.

Come on all mankind! Wake up and do your duty,. Start serving the only true God. Awake and take up your wedding garment! The groom will soon be here; do you have on the wedding garment or not?

When the groom appears, I want to be a bride ready for my lover Jesus Christ who takes me to that mansion which he has gone to prepare.

Upon planning our wedding over sixty-four years ago, my wife and I were planning to live in a reasonably good room in those days. However, there was a disappointment. We did not get that room, and I lost weight fretting because I was not able to take my new bride to a comfortable accommodation.

Her father had a house and wanted us to move in with him, but I did not want to go and live with her father at the time. I wanted to show that I was a responsible man.

Many years ago, the country of my birth held a general election. The campaign slogan of one of the political party's was, "Time for a Change." We need to make changes in our lives in whatever we do. As a driver, you need to change gears, or you may be stopped by a police officer.

Some years ago, while driving home from work, I was driving slowly and was stopped by the police, I was asked why I was driving so slowly, and I told him I had just finished a fourteen-hour shift at work. I was again asked, "Were you drinking?" I replied, "No. I am a minister of religion, I do not take strong drinks." There were more than one officer, and they offered to accompany me home, but I told them I would be okay.

Be reasonable both to yourself and others. Would you be happy to see your children in paradise while you are in hell, or the other way round?

Unless you make that decision to change the way you are living, surely, you will be going to hell. The same goes for me if I do not continue to live a good Christian life.

You may say "I am not a Christian, but I am living a better life than they are..."

That's their problem, not yours. They will have to give an account for themselves.

While living in my birth country, one night I heard someone say I was the only true believer in my church. The person did not know I heard her. Yes, I tried to live a good Christian life, but that did not make me the only one living a good life. Surely there were others, but the person picked me out. What man sees is not what God sees. Man looks on the outside, but God looks on the heart. I do love our God and his son Jesus Christ, and I am encouraging you to do the same.

Please take time and consider your way of living, there are two roads, make your choice.

In the marriage vows, we say "For better for worse... till death us do part." Why not now say,

"I have wandered away from God. I have done things that I should not have done, but now I will change my ways and accept Jesus Christ as my redeemer. I do the things that He

wants me to do, and what He does not want me to do, I will do them no more. I accept him now and I promise to serve him all the days of my life."

It would be one of the best things that you could do. I made that choice over seventy years ago, and it was the best thing that I have ever done.

CHAPTER 31

When the Roll is Called...

Come and join with me and others who are waiting for that grand day when we shall arise from death (or still alive), going to yonder land of glory.

Some years ago, I heard a preacher say that the reason Jesus did not know when the end of time is, was because He loved us so much that His Father did not tell Him, or He would have told us.

According to the Holy Book, not even the Son knows when He will return. All we know is that He told us while He was on earth that He will be coming back to receive His own.

At about the age of four, my great grandmother died, I still remember one song that was sung: "When the roll is called up yonder, I will be there.

We do not know when He shall appear, but one thing we do know is that He will soon be here. Jesus Christ will be coming back soon, and it is my duty to sound the alarm, He will be coming back, not as baby, but as a King, and the mercy door will be closed.

We are all duly warned to repent of our sins and start serving the Almighty God. It is of no good If I try and play down the matter. Jesus Christ will be coming back Get. Get your house in order,

If I was with you, I could have prayed with you and hope you would make a decision, but I may never know you. One thing I do know: I will be there in heaven because the old account was settled when I surrendered my life to God.

I am requesting you to join me to pray. Please close your eyes and pray with me.

"*Heavenly Father, I give you praise allowing me to be alive this day. I am weak, but thou art strong. Please Lord Jesus, I know and hear of your goodness towards all mankind. I understand that without you, my life has no meaning. Lord, I am willing to give my life to you this day, and I make this promise to serve you for the rest of my life.*

Oh God, I heard you love us so much that you sent your only Son to die for me, and I thank you for what you have done for me and all mankind. I heard of your Son's death on the cross over two thousand years ago, shedding his blood to set me free

from sin. Help me God to love you as you do love me, and at the end you will help me to take my flight to that mansion that your son has promised to come back to receive us into.

Your love is everlasting, help me to continue loving you until the day I die, then I know you will receive me into your Kingdom forever.

Thank you, Lord."

CHAPTER 32

On My Way to Glory Land

My first book was titled, *Walking with God in this troubled world.* Life is full of so much trouble. Those that have passed on would not want to come back in this life. I have been to the outpatient department several times, and people just keep coming in sick. At one time I spent over twelve hours in the A&E department.

I have been in the United Kingdom nearly seventy years, and going to the bank to withdraw or deposit money is like going to a third world country; the queues are so long.

Before, you could see three or four different banks in your locality. Now, people must travel far away to withdraw or deposit their funds. At the end of the financial year, the banks declare a profit of millions of pounds, but they paid you peanuts in interest on your savings.

I cannot tell you why I write in this manner, but the Spirit of God is upon me.

There ought to be a change in the way things are today. We cannot go on as it is. Both governments and the citizens will have to come together and work as one people to get things done properly in the sight of God.

Sound the alarm, preachers! God is not happy, and He is going to do something about it.

We need good Christian leaders to lead God's people into godly living. Any nation that forgets God is in a very serious condition.

Our Heavenly Father does not like rebellious nations. If a nation is not living as God intended them to, He does not take it lightly. According to records long before I was born, God dealt with nations that rebelled against Him severely.

In the Bible, we are told about the flood in Noah's days, and also Sodom and Gomorrah. What God did to those nations in the past, He will do again, and it could be sooner than we believe.

Wake up, people! Arise from the dead and seek God before it is too late.

Any nation or people who forsake the living God is in great danger. Do not be like fools that do not accept the one who made them.

"Can you put the stars or moon in the sky? Can you dry up the Red Sea and let the people cross on dry

land? Do you know the number of hairs on your head? Do you know how many fish are in the sea? Do you really know when my Son Jesus Christ will return to earth? If you do know, stay as you are; but a day is coming when your records of what you have done on earth will be shown to you, and what will your answer be?"

Are you washed in the blood of the lamb, are your garments clean and ready for the groom? What will your answer be? Are you ready for the judgement call? You better get ready for the day of His coming. If I were you, I would surely take action because, what you are reading is from a ninety-one-year-old man who is on his way to glory land.

I just do not want to be here much longer!

When my father took ill, I heard that some church members went to pray for him at home. A church brother promised him, "I will be coming to visit you tomorrow." My father replied, "Do not come and look for me tomorrow. I won't be here. I will be going home." He died just after midnight.

What a testimony!

I wish I could hear him pray in that deep voice again!

I am waiting for that time to come for me to go home to my parents and other loved ones. When that time comes, I shall be ready to take my flight to that heavenly home.

I will surely miss my loved ones and people who have been very kind to me and have shown great love. Some have gone home to be with their maker and others are still with us. I hope to meet them then sit beside our Jesus and tell Him, "Satan did me harm, but I thank You for dying for me on the cross." What a day that will be!

We are going home to be with Him forever: no more pain, no more sickness and certainly no more dying. We will be free as birds! Yes, it will be a great day for the ransomed.

I have a home prepared for me in glory land. There won't be any rent or mortgage to pay because Jesus Christ the Son of God has paid it all.

Such a loving God He is! He is a very good God. For over seventy years, I have experienced His love and care. He is such a loving Father to all mankind and He will take great care of you. He is truly the best friend you could have.

I heard of a woman who said God is so good to her that people would wonder if He was having an affair with her. It sounds silly, but that's the way she felt about God! Some people still feel that Jesus Christ was having an affair with Mary and Martha, the two sisters, because He used to go and spent time with them.

When my wife and I went to visit the Holy Land, we went to the home where they were living while Jesus was on earth. As we were walking on this road, it felt so good knowing that Jesus Christ had walked the same road.

The district is one of the poorest parts of the Holy Land, but our Saviour chose to go there and and have sweet communion with these two sisters and their brother Lazarus whom He raised from the dead.

Many of us have good spouses, but sometimes they get on our nerves don't they? The reason for this is that we are all human. Job's wife got on his nerves when she told him, "Curse God and die". This poor woman saw that her beloved husband had lost everything. She became depressed and sorrowful about what had happened to her family.

With wisdom, Job replied, "You speak like a foolish woman." That was what King David said in the Psalms: anyone who says there is no God is a fool (Psalm 14:1).

O how good our loving God is! He cares for his people. When you are hurt, He too is hurt. There is no need to worry or fret. He knows our cry and He hears us all. We only need to have faith in Him, and that He will hear us when we cry out to Him. He will come and deliver us from all harm.

There will be joy unspeakable when our Saviour returns to take His chosen ones to be with Him and His Father. They are in one accord, they have sweet communion, and the Son will never do anything that is not His Father's will.

Not too long ago I visited my place of birth and saw the lovely homes someone built in preparation for retirement, but the owner had gone home to their maker. You see, this earth is not our home. You and I will be going either to heaven or hell when we die or if we are alive on the Lord's return.

Build your treasures up in heaven, my dear friend. You will not be allowed to take anything you have in this world. You could tell the administrator of your will to put all your earthly gains in your coffin when you die; but you won't even know if he or she did what you said.

When my father died, I wanted to see him in the mortuary before the funeral and asked my cousin to go with me. He asked, "Are you sure you want to go?" I said yes. When I saw my father's dead body, I was shocked. His human remains were like that of a dead cat!

What is man? We are just dust. A tree has more hope than us wicked sinners. You might dress nicely in a respectable suit or dress and have a good job, but you are going to die one day, and your body will just be like my father's.

The grave is a place for dead bodies. However, there is hope beyond the grave.

I recall having a critical person in our church that I had to deal with. She was the church clerk and she would criticise everything you did. It got so bad that I did not want to do anything in the church.

Not long after, she left the church. People like that need another touch of Jesus Christ; a double portion of the blood of our saviour. Do not let such people get you down. Love them and pray for them, but don't be too close to them. If they are of Christ, they will stay; but if they are of man, they will fade away.

Someone tried to remind me of what I used to do before. I replied "Yes, I am guilty as charged, but the blood of Jesus Christ has covered them all."

The things I have done in the past, I made a promise never to do them anymore. I have forgotten the past and moved on. All my sins have been washed away by the blood of Jesus, the Son of God, and He remembers them no more. My past debts have been all paid off and should be forgotten, I will also remember them no more, because the blood of the Lamb has covered them all.

The future is looking brighter every day as I travel along. I am on my way to take my flight to glory land, where the sun will always shine.

Leave the bad things of this world and join with me to sing the songs of peace and love. That's where I want to be!

Better days are coming by and by. Give your burdens to the one who cleansed the leper, raised the dead and fed the hungry.

When I was around 13 or 14 years old, some boys and I were playing marble on the main road, and the post man was coming on his bike. All the other boys moved to the side bank to give way to the postman, because you should not hold up the king or queen on the motorway, I did not move back as the other boys, and the postman got hold of me and gave me a good belting. My loving mother saw what happened, and she said "Serves you right! I told you not to play on the street."

If it was for something less trivial, and that post man used his belt on me, she probably would have gone to prison for what he had done, you just do not touch mama's son.

If I had died and gone to hell after my mother passed away many years ago, she probably would have said, "Poor thing! He should have known better, because I did send him to Sunday School when he was a child."

There won't be any special treatment for anyone. No matter how they try, the wicked will not escape the fire of hell.

It for this reason that I am beseeching you to run for your life. Do not let the devil get hold of you. If he does, he is going to hold on to you with brute force, and no way is he going to let you loose. The evil man is very dangerous, keep away from him at all costs, my friend.

There is going to be grand day up in heaven. All the patriarchs of old will be there: Abraham will be there; King David, Moses and the apostles of Jesus will be there - including Paul who at a time persecuted the Christians. Peter who claimed that he did not know Jesus, which was a lie - they all will be in heaven. Don't you want to be there? Most of those that I have mentioned above were both murderers, liars, and adulterers, but they repented of their sins.

The blood of Jesus Christ is powerful to wash away your sins as well.

Open the door of your heart. Open and let God in.

"Come home, come home," says the Lord.

"Come home and have supper with me, because I am your God. Do not have any other God beside me because I am a jealous God. Come home and be at peace.'

"My burden is light and my love is forever and forever. Come home and dine with me. My angels are waiting to welcome you home. You have strayed away from my presence

far too long. Come home! You are my child and I sincerely love you. You were a sinner doomed to die, but because of my love, I sent my only Son to die for you.

"Heaven's doors are waiting to open for my angels to welcome you home. Do not linger. Do not wait. The heavenly door will soon to be shut, and when it is shut no man can open the door.

"Why wait, my weary child? Come home and have rest for your soul. Come home and put on your garment, your shining crown and shoes.

"Leave your earthly garments and come to me while time is on your side. The blessings are waiting for all those that surrender their lives to me. Do not wait until tomorrow. It may never be yours.

"Waiting is very dangerous. Do not wait any longer while the sun shines. There were some who were waiting for another day, but they did not make it because their time had gone. So take up your cross and follow me, and you will have sweet rest.

"My only Son has made you a promise to give you a mansion in my heavenly home and that promise is forever.

"There is no need for you to bring your earthly vessels. Your golden ones are waiting for you, my child.

"Make up your mind to follow me and I will give you rest for your soul. Come and put on your wedding garments that the groom has bought for you. My angels are waiting to welcome you home.

"Tarry no longer, you have waited too long, all waiting will be over when heaven's door is closed. You have wasted many

years making up your mind, I encourage you not to wait very much longer.

"Your burden is heavy and my burden is light. Get ready book your flight for that heavenly home, where the heavenly host is waiting to welcome you to your heavenly home.

"You can have no better friend than my only Son who gave his life for you. Be courageous and book your heavenly flight to take you home to glory land."

CHAPTER 33

Heaven-Bound

God bless you for taking time out to read my book. I do hope you have been blessed.

Encourage others to get copies, too. Let them go and buy oil for themselves. Do not stop reading this book, it has been written from the heart and in love.

Share the good news with others that God and His son are real, and they are full of love for everyone - no matter the nation or tribe. Even when you are committing sin, they still love you, it is just the sin they do not love.

Have you ever done some good to someone and they turned out to be ungrateful to you? I have, and it surely did hurt.

In spite of all things that God has done for all men, we can sometimes be ungrateful by not remembering those things.

I love what my mother taught me when I was a very young child. If someone does you one good and ninety-nine wrongs, just remember the good. That is some good advice from a loving mother!

When I think about Him and all He has done for me, my heart cries out, 'Thank you!" He has rescued me from my sin and shame. He has heard my cry and delivered me from my enemies and from the cold. How could I do without Him?

I was sinking fast, but the lifeboat came and rescued me. Thank God for sending His angel to save me when I was doomed to die, but the lifeboat came and rescued me. There is no friend in this whole wide world like Jesus Christ.

I will linger no more, I go to my father and will say,

"I am sorry for the sins I committed, please forgive me of all the bad things I have done. I will never do the things I did anymore, knowing they were wrong. Help me to be faithful to you. Lord Jesus, take me and lead me onto the promised land where we will not die, or never will stray away from your presence."

What a day that will be when all tears are gone and I am now free to wear my crown. Heaven bells are ringing joyously that a sinner has come to have rest and sweet peace.

How beautiful it will be when I see my earthly brothers and sisters all wearing that shining crown! My heavenly crown I shall wear when I get home to be with friends and all those who were washed in the blood of the lamb, Jesus Christ,

He says, *"I have given my life for you. What have you given for me?"*

My mother used to say there is a cross for Jesus, and there is one for me too. My fellow men and women run for your life, run to Jesus Christ who gave his life for you, run.

Eighty years ago, the British won the Second World War, During the war, I remember I was in the kitchen when the church bell rang, letting us know all lights should be turned off. Cars had to drive without lights, it was very scary, but thank God I am alive to tell the younger generation what it was like during the second world war.

Let's celebrate and give thanks for His goodness to us. Run to Jesus! Book your flight on this heaven-bound plane.

I would rather have Jesus than anything else. He is a friend indeed!

Printed in Dunstable, United Kingdom

68762020R00077